The *Essence* of Life

The *Essence* of Life

Motilal Oswal

Ocean Paperbacks

A Division of Ocean Books Pvt. Ltd.

ISO 9001:2008 Publishers

Published by
Ocean Paperbacks
A Division of Ocean Books Pvt. Ltd.
4/19 Asaf Ali Road,
New Delhi-110 002 (INDIA)
e-mail: info@oceanbooks.in

ISBN 978-81-8430-144-1
The Essence of Life
by **Motilal Oswal**

Edition
First, 2012

Price
Rs. 150.00 (Rs. One Hundred Fifty only)

Printed at
Bhanu Printers, Delhi

This book is especially dedicated to my lovely children—Pratiksha and Pratik.

They are life's best gift to me. I would like to share with them the goodies of life.

I am sure they would be enriched by this treasure trove of quotes!

Preface

In the recent past, I published a book of quotes -*The Essence of Business and Management*. This book included a few of my own thoughts and other quotes – all acquired by reading and day-to-day practical experience.

The *Essence of Business and Management* and a book *entitled Wealth Creation Thoughts* by my co-promoter, Raamdeo Agrawal, cover two aspects—business and capital markets.

A book of quotes on the very topic of LIFE will make this a complete collection. Hence, this book!

I have had my share of good and tough experiences in the last 48 years, and learned some precious lessons in the process. I have travelled a lot, met and interacted with many people. I have been continuously reading and reflecting on life and business. All of this has shaped me and the contents of this book.

I share not only the quotes but a few thoughts on all the themes or quote-categories in this book. This will enable the readers to not just read, but feel the quotes in the way they have touched my life.

Quotes are powerful. Just a few words capture so much truth and wisdom. They are highly impactful. They have the power to motivate and spur us on. They impose laser-like focus on our thinking and guide us. Over the years, I have had the pleasure of sharing such quotes with many people; and they have made a lasting impact all round. To this day, I continue this daily ritual of lighting up minds with quotes.

Why daily? This again can be answered by a quote. As Zig Ziglar said "People often say that motivation doesn't last. Well, neither does bathing—that's why we recommend it daily." Well said!

I would like to appreciate the efforts put in by Ramnik Chhabra, Hari Krishnan and Kejal Tolia of our team.

I am sure this book will add value to your life. I look forward to your feedback as well.

Thank you,

Motilal Oswal

Contents

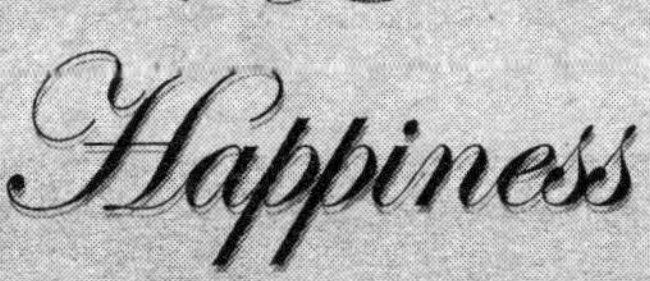

Happiness

In today's 'fast forward' life, when we hear the words 'Happy Birthday' and 'Happy New Year', we realize that they are just pleasant verbal exchanges. True depth of meaning and feeling is missing. Isn't it?

Life is stressful and complicated and makes us miserable. Or is there something within us that makes things miserable? Are we making life difficult and complicated for ourselves?

All of us wish for happiness and peace. But what will get us there? Many think it is material possessions. Many are caught in the 'If-then' mode ("If only I had so-and-so, then I would be happy"). And so, they postpone happiness in the rush for new wants and wishes.

People often put the cart before the horse. We can equate the horse to 'being happy' and the cart is 'things we want'. We think that once we get things we want we'll be happy. But happiness comes first. It empowers us to acquire the rest.

Good health, good relationships and positive thoughts are the only prerequisites for happiness.

Sometimes we do get it right, and are happy. But the happiness is short lived. We chase it away and rejoin the rat-race.

My daughter became a doctor after five years of focus and hard work. When the results came in, we were overjoyed! But in a few days, we let go of the immediate joy and went into planning mode to better her career.

We also let small irritants cast a shadow over the big moments. Jealousy, comparisons and unreal expectations cause a lot of harm. Don't sweat the small stuff! Treasure good things, good memories and let go of the rest. True happiness comes from within, and does not lie outside of us. We can create a mind set full of positive thoughts. Count our blessings and enjoy the simple joy of being alive!

We are responsible for our own happiness.

Happiness

The key to happiness is not that you
never get angry, upset, frustrated,
irritated or depressed;
it's how fast you get out
of all this nonsense

We tend to forget that happiness doesn't come
as a result of getting something we don't have,
but it rather comes by recognizing and
appreciating all that we have
~ Frederick Keonig ~

■

Happiness is a perfume which
you cannot pour on someone without
getting some on yourself
~ Ralph Waldo Emerson ~

■

Happiness is the result of a healthy body,
positive thoughts and balanced emotions

■

The best and most beautiful things in the world
cannot be seen or even touched,
they must be felt with the heart
~ Helen Keller ~

■

The purpose of life is not to be happy. It is to be useful,
to be honorable, to be compassionate, to have it
make some difference that you have lived and lived well
~ Ralph Waldo Emerson ~

■

The key to happiness is having dreams...
the key to success is making them come true
~ James Allen ~

Hurting someone is as easy as
cutting a tree within a moment.
But making someone happy is like
growing a tree.
It takes a lot of time, care & patience

Happiness is when what you think, what you say, and what you do are in harmony

~ Mahatma Gandhi ~

■

The happiness in my life depends
on the quality of my thoughts

■

Spend a day shifting the focus from seeking love
and appreciation to offering love and appreciation
and it automatically will be the
happiest day of your life

■

Heart is not a dustbin to dump
all the worries of your life!
It is a golden pot for collection of
sweet moments of your life!

■

Close your mouth, quiet your desires
and your life will be full and healthy.
Keep talking and meddling in the affairs
of the world and your life will be beyond hope

~ Lao Tzu ~

There is no road in the world that goes to happiness...but happiness can take you anywhere in the world

Happiness depends on what you can give,
not on what you can get
~ Swami Chinmayananda ~

■

If you want to maximize your happiness,
then make a habit to share your happiness

■

Want to make your home, workplace or community a happier place? Start by being happy yourself and your happiness will be contagious.
~ Lucy MacDonald ~

■

Mind is the most powerful thing in the world.
One who has controlled his mind can
control anything in the world
~ Swami Vivekananda ~

■

Nothing lasts forever - the present moment of
joy and sorrow will soon pass away

■

Heaven has two gates, humility and contentment.
Hell has two gates, pride and greed

■

The result of anger is always more painful
than the reason for anger

Health

Walking and Exercise have been a part of my life for the last 24 years. It has now become a passion with me. This fitness regime includes yoga too. Sure, it requires a lot of discipline and motivation. Early morning, there are people in the jogging park. Only about 5% of the population is pro-actively into fitness activity. Many people turn to walking, jogging and yoga only when a doctor advises or a health problem causes them to.

These same people religiously do the maintenance of their cars, homes and offices; but spare no time or thought for their own bodies.

Most human beings wish for better health, but are not able to act on their wish. 'Knowing' and 'Doing' are two different things. Many people worsen their health by doing undesirable things in spite of knowing the result of their actions. They prioritize other things and health falls by the wayside.

On a deeper level, it is true that a healthy mind can only reside in a healthy body. Positive thoughts, good relationships and a stress-free environment often come from good health.

Health Management is the combination of physical fitness and diet. I came across a book by Rujuta Divekar, Don't Lose Your Mind, Lose Your Weight'. The book made me change my food habits and positively enhanced my health and wellbeing. But one must be careful not to overdo the fitness bit. My injuries due to over-enthusiastic squash and marathon running sessions remind me of that!

Laughter is such a positive daily vitamin for good health. A very powerful stress-buster!

God has given us 24 hours in a day. Surely, we can invest 30 minutes of the day in taking care of our health. The investment will yield disproportionate returns. We need to 'just do it'!

Age is an issue of mind over matter.
If you don't mind, it does not matter
~ Mark Twain ~

So many people spend their health gaining wealth,
and then have to spend their wealth
to regain their health
~ Reb Materi ~

■

Stubborn people suffer much

■

Two things are bad for the heart
– running uphill and running down people
~ Bernard Baruch ~

■

First half of our life we try to
gain wealth and lose our health;
Second half of our life we
spend wealth to regain our health

■

I can use weight as an indicator of what else is
going right or wrong in my life.
So when I start adding a few pounds,
I start paying attention to what that means in other areas
~ Charles Garfield ~

■

So many men – and increasingly more women – bear
tremendous physical demands and
elevated levels of stress. Their bodies warn them

My fat scares me—it's a ticking time bomb

~ Carrie Latet ~

It's well documented that there's a correlation between your fitness and not only your performance but also basic things like self-esteem, self-love, self-acceptance.
~ Charles Garfield ~

■

Best doctors in the world:
sunlight, water, rest, air, exercise,
diet, family, self-confidence

■

Those who believe that they do not have time for exercise, must understand that sooner or later, they will have to give time to sickness

■

Just like our bodies need food everyday, our minds need positive thoughts everyday
~ Shiv Khera ~

■

Every human being is the author of his own health or disease
~ Buddha ~

■

Your body is the baggage you must carry through life. The more excess the baggage, the shorter the trip
~ Arnold H. Glasgow ~

Relationships

Relationships create meaning in our life. Our bonds with our parents, siblings, business associates, team members are very special. But we often start taking them for granted. We do not nurture them. This is ironic because our Indian culture gives great importance to relationships as compared ιo the western world; where people are lonely and alienated.

Relationships take an entire life to build, nurture and maintain; but only a few seconds to break. They can neither be bought nor sold.

I have seen many successful people build big businesses on the foundation of very strong relationships. And I have seen some struggle simply because they were unable to hold on to their relationships.

We need to have the mindset of a giver instead of a taker. 'Giving' gives us credibility. The beauty of life is that when we give, we receive many times over. Genuine caring and giving builds life-long relationships.

I am in touch with my school friends and distant relatives. Our family is a close-knit one. I always make an effort to reach out and be in touch with colleagues and friends. I wish around two thousand people every year on their special occasions; be it birthdays or anniversaries. I send thank-you cards, share books, articles, mails, and quotes with many of them. I derive a lot of pleasure and intense satisfaction from being connected.

My experience tells me that the best way to manage relationships is to appreciate people, be honest with them; and have an attitude of giving and utmost humility.

How do we do that? By connecting with our real self and by listening. Listening is an extremely powerful binding force for relationships. Personal meetings and direct communications strengthen them further.

Laughter is the shortest distance
between two people
~ Victor Borge ~

Keep away from people who try to
be little your ambitions
~ Mark Twain ~

■

The more arguments we win,
the lesser friends we will have

■

A lot of trouble would disappear if people
talk "to" one another, instead of "about" one another

■

A wise man is one who forgets the faults of others,
but always remembers his own

■

People are made to be loved and things
are made to be used.
The confusion in the world is people
are being used and things are being loved

■

Never tell your problems to anyone except
your dear ones. Because 20% people don't care and
the other 80% people are glad that you have problems
~ Aristotle ~

Through saying those three simple words,
"I forgive you," lives and relationships
have been dramatically saved
again and again
~ John Gray ~

I have never gone to sleep with a grievance against
anyone. And, as far as I could,
I have never let anyone go to sleep
with a grievance against me
~ Abba Agathon ~

■

When we don't forgive in one relationship,
our love is restricted in all our relationships
~ John Gray ~

■

People will forget what you said, people will forget
what you did, but people will never forget
how you made them feel
~ Maya Angelou ~

■

You can make more friends by becoming
interested in other people than you can
by trying to get people interested in you
~ Dale Carnegie ~

■

The quality of your life is the quality of
your relationships
~ Anthony Robbins ~

■

Do not impose on others what you yourself do not desire
~ Confucius ~

Most happy couples rarely have the same
character and understanding.
They just make the best of their differences
~ **Anonymous** ~

Truth of life: "Never play with the feelings of others."
Because you may win the game
but the risk is that you will surely lose the person

■

Be known as someone with a cool head,
warm heart and great character

■

You are great if you can find your faults.
Greater if you can remove/reduce them.
But you are the greatest if you accept &
love others with their faults

■

Family, health, friends and spirit:
these things don't come with a price tag.
But when we lose them, we realize the cost

■

A single finger which wipes out your tears
in your bad time is much better than
ten fingers which join hands & clap in your victory

■

Being good to people is somewhat similar to being a
goalkeeper. No matter how many goals you save,
people only remember the one you missed!

Leave your kids enough to do anything,
but not enough to do nothing!
~ **Warren Buffet** ~

We get comfort from those who agree with us,
but we get growth from only those who don't

■

"People are not difficult, people are different."
If we understand this fact, we can build
great relationships and avoid many sour relationships

■

Life has made me realize that what is valuable
is not "what" I have in my life,
but "who" I have in my life

■

Forgiveness has nothing to do with whether someone
deserves to be forgiven
- it is an act of love, not of justice

■

You never pay attention to a part of your body
till it pains. Don't let it happen in your relationships

■

Find some time for the dear ones in your life.
Else one day you will find time but not the dear ones

■

It's better to lose your ego to the one you love than
to lose the one you love because of ego

If you educate a man
you educate a person,
but if you educate a woman,
you educate a family

What we leave 'in' our children, is more important than what we leave 'for' our children

■

Failure also looks beautiful, when you have a loved one to support you.
Success also hurts, when you don't have a loved one to wish you

■

Believing everybody is dangerous;
believing nobody is very dangerous
~ Abraham Lincoln ~

■

When a man points a finger at someone else, he should remember that three of his fingers are pointing at himself

■

Bees that have honey in mouth have stings in their tails. So be careful with those who pretend to be sweet

■

The bitter hard reality of life is that when you need advice, everyone is ready to help you, but when you need help, everyone is ready to advise you

Wealth

In this materialistic world, people spend disproportionate time and effort to acquire wealth. Money is given prime importance at the cost of our health, relationships and values.

Yes, wealth is very important; but it is not everything. No amount of wealth is enough for people in blind pursuit of it. Many relationships have been broken by the lure of gold.

My experience is that you don't have to compromise on your health, relationships, and values. Sure enough, if we take care of them, we actually are in a position to gain sustainable wealth! No shortcuts will do. A sense of balance and appreciation for the finer aspects of life is the only way.

After all, what is the point of having wealth if you don't give time to family? What is the point in having wealth if you fall sick every week? What is the point in having wealth if you are not enjoying your kids' company? Or that of your loved ones? What is the point in having wealth if you don't care for society?

There are so many people who have wealth, but very few people who really enjoy it.

Let me also share that earning wealth and investing wealth are two distinct activities and require different skill sets. Very few people are good at both.

Your most expensive advice is the free advice you receive from your financially struggling friends/relatives

~ Robert Kiyosaki ~

If you are born poor, it's not your mistake,
but if you die poor, it's your mistake
~ Bill Gates ~

■

Too many people spend money they haven't earned,
to buy things they don't want,
to impress people they don't like
~ Will Rogers ~

■

Money will buy me a house, but not a home;
a bed but not a good nights sleep;
a companion but not a friend;
a good time but not peace of mind
~ Zig Ziglar ~

■

There is only one class of people that thinks
more about money than the rich and that is the poor.
In fact, the poor can think of nothing else
~ Deepak Chopra ~

■

When money talks, there are few interruptions
~ Herbert V. Prochnow ~

■

Do not focus on how to spend less money,
instead, focus on how to earn more money to spend
~ Ratan Tata ~

Always remember, money isn't everything, but make sure that you've made lots of it before talking such nonsense

~ Bill Gates ~

Being rich is having money,
being wealthy is having time

■

Silver in the hair is respected only when
gold is in the pocket

■

Money is an excellent servant, but a horrible master
~ P. T. Barnum ~

■

There is no amount of money in the world
that will make you comfortable
if you are not comfortable with yourself.
~ Stuart Wilde ~

■

Keep my hand outside the coffin,
so that the world knows that the one who won the
world had nothing in hand when he died
~ Alexander ~

Career

I have seen many people who think and behave as if life is work and work is life. They eat, sleep, and drink work, work and only work.

Such an approach is fine if you have made peace with yourself that work is the only thing that matters and you truly enjoy work. Indeed, goal clarity is indispensable for career-success. But, that is often not the case. Many individuals are drifting through their careers and do not succeed. What takes us far is focusing on priorities, team building and effective delegation.

If not managed well, work negatively affects health, relationships and our fulfillment. We need to reflect when that happens.

Let us remind ourselves that LIFE is much, much bigger than work. Work, after all is just one aspect of life. Our health, our emotional well-being and happiness, our relationships—they are the more important aspects.

There was this tragic news of a young multinational CEO who passed away suddenly at the very young age of forty-two. Sleep-deprivation and a highly demanding work routine might have played a major role in nipping such a promising career in its bud.

Indeed, work-related tensions are rising and they harm health in a big way.

I work hard; but have taken adequate care to see that work doesn't come at the cost of family time, vacations, fitness programs, diet discipline and reading time.

We must also differentiate between activity and productivity. Stress and burn-out happens when we are stuck in mundane activities. We must be mindful of this distinction and keep a sense of proportion.

An important attribute of successful people is their impatience with negative thinking and negative acting people

He who stops being better, stops being good

~ Oliver Cromwell ~

■

Winners recognize their limitations
but focus on their strengths.
Losers know their strengths
but focus on their weaknesses

■

A man is not paid for having a head and hands,
but for using them

~ Elbert Hubbard ~

■

There are no short cuts to any place worth going

~ Beverly Sills ~

■

If you do what you've always done,
you'll get what you've always gotten

~ Anthony Robbins ~

■

Most people decide emotionally and then
justify logically

I have never in my life learned anything
from any person who agreed with me
~ Warren Buffet ~

If you find yourself in a hole, the first thing to do is stop digging

~ Will Rogers ~

■

Everything you want is just outside your comfort zone

~ Robert Allen ~

■

We judge ourselves by what we feel capable of doing, while others judge us by what we have already done

~ Henry Wordsworth ~

■

H . A . L . T. Method for a successful life:
Never make a decision when you are—
Hungry, Angry, Lonely or Tired!

■

There are four kinds of people:
those who make things happen;
those who watch things happen;
those who wonder what happened;
and those who don't know that anything happened!

~ Mary Kay Ash ~

■

Lack of confidence is born from a lack of preparation

~ Shannon Wilburn ~

Goals & Vision

In my orientation address to new associates, I invariably end up asking them – what are your goals? Quite a few answers are vague. The thinking behind the answers is muddled or wishful thinking.

A fact of life is that very few people have well-defined goals. Only 3% of people on this earth have well-defined, written goals. Goal-setting – the process of getting crystal-clear clarity on goals—is the most critical activity for individuals and organizations.

Without goals, you are like a football! Everyone is kicking you and you are at the mercy of others. Goals create a definite purpose in life. They stimulate a positive change by giving a sense of direction. We know where to go and stride confidently into the future.

Without goals, we are like a ship adrift in the ocean—dull and motionless.

Goals have to be SMART—Smart, Measurable, Achievable, Realistic and Time-bound. It has become a cliché – accepted but not practiced.

Goals should also make us stretch as only then will we build capability and surpass our limits. We have to think big and get out of our comfort zone.

When I was studying at the higher secondary level, my goal was to be a chartered accountant. I achieved my goal and became one. When we started the broking business, there were thousands of brokers in the industry. Yet, we ambitiously set for ourselves a goal of being at the very top in this competitive space. We achieved that within twenty years.

The beauty about goals is that there is always something to look forward to and achieve.

Speed is useful only if you are running in the right direction

~ Joel Barker ~

It is not the mountain we conquer, but ourselves
~ Sir Edmund Hillary ~

■

By recording your dreams and goals on paper,
you set in motion the process of
becoming the person you want to be
~ Mark Victor Hansen ~

■

The greater danger for most of us is not that
our aim is too high and we miss it, but
that it is too low and we hit it
~ Michelangelo ~

■

Whatever the mind of man can conceive
and believe, it can achieve
~ Napoleon Hill ~

■

You see things and say, 'Why?', but I dream
things and say, 'Why not?'
~ George Bernard Shaw ~

■

Shoot for the moon. Even if you miss,
you'll land among the stars
~ Les Brown ~

There are no limits to what you can accomplish except for the limits you place on your own imagination. And since there are no limits to what you can imagine, there are no limits to what you can achieve

~ Brian Tracy ~

Don't decrease your goal to the extent of your ability, increase your ability to the extent of your goal

■

I've had dreams and I've had nightmares.
I've overcome my nightmares because of my dreams
~ Jonas Salk ~

■

The person who chases two rabbits catches neither
~ Confucius ~

■

People with goals succeed because they know where they're going
~ Earl Nightingale ~

■

With goals you fly like an arrow, straight and true to your target

■

A person with a clear purpose will make progress on even the roughest road.
A person with no purpose will make no progress on even the smoothest road
~ Thomas Carlyle ~

Begin with the end in mind
~ **Dr. Stephen Covey** ~

Obstacles are those frightful things
you see when you take your eyes off your goal
~ Henry Ford ~

■

People never reach their goals because they
never set them in the first place.
They spend more time planning
a vacation than they do planning their own lives
~ Denis Waitley ~

■

The me I see is the me I will be

■

Think big, think fast, think ahead.
Ideas are no one's monopoly,
you do not require an invitation to make profits
~ Dhirubhai Ambani ~

■

Even if I don't reach all my goals,
I've still gone higher than I would have,
if I hadn't set any

■

A goal without a deadline is not a goal but
it is a wish

You are never too old to set another goal or
to dream a new dream

~ Les Brown ~

If you can't fly, run. If you can't run, walk.
If you can't walk, crawl.
But whatever you do,
keep moving towards your goal
~ Martin Luther King ~

■

The world has the habit of making room for
the man whose actions
show that he knows where he is going
~ Napoleon Hill ~

■

It doesn't matter where you are coming from.
All that matters is where you are going
~ Brian Tracy ~

■

It is more important to know where you
are going than to get there quickly.
Do not mistake activity for achievement
~ Mabel Newcomber ~

■

Show me a thoroughly satisfied man and
I will show you a failure
~ Patti Hathaway ~

Self-Motivation

I love the saying 'Where there is a will, there is a way'.

In our organization, we always look out for people who are self-starters. Self-starters demand and take higher responsibilities and get the freedom to fulfill them. They are action-oriented and proactive. They are passionate about what they do; and are bouncing with high energy all over the place!

The contrast between them and reactive people is eye-opening. You have to continuously push reactive people. And we don't like to push!

I come from a very small village in Rajasthan on the border of Pakistan. My father was a grain merchant. But, I was self-motivated to do something else; to be on my own. And that led me to where I am today. Similarly, it was her self-motivation that led my daughter to take up medicine.

It is self-motivation that drives people to achieve. Come to think of it, the external push, the external motivation may or may not come. Why do we wait? What if nothing happens?

We should raise the bar continuously, inch by inch, on our own. And ignore the naysayer; the negative person.

I have faced many problems and challenges in my career; and it is my fighting spirit that has pulled me through.

I have found that self-motivation is the biggest motivation; resulting in miracles.

I have not failed.
I've just found 10,000 ways that won't work
~ Thomas Edison ~

Luck is what happens when
preparation meets opportunity
~ Seneca ~

■

People often say that motivation doesn't last.
Well, neither does bathing
that's why we recommend it daily
~ Zig Ziglar ~

■

To reach any significant goal you must leave your comfort zone. We have either physical comfort zones or we develop mental, emotional, social or psychological comfort zones
~ Hyrum W. Smith ~

■

Motivation alone is not enough. If you have an idiot and you motivate him, now you have a motivated idiot
~ Jim Rohn ~

■

When you do anything new at first, people may laugh at
you then they may challenge you,
then they'll watch you succeed and
then they'll wish they were you!

■

I may be walking slowly, but I never walk backwards and whenever I walk backwards, its for a long jump
~ Carl Lewis ~

If one can do it, you too can do it. If none can do it, you must do it

~ Japanese proverb ~

Conquer yourself and the world
lies at your feet
~ Augustine ~

■

The greatest glory in living
lies not in never falling,
but in rising every time we fall
~ Nelson Mandela ~

■

If you have the will to win, you have achieved
half your success; If you don't, you
have achieved half your failure
~ David Ambrose ~

■

Motivation is what gets you started.
Habit is what keeps you going
~ Jim Rohn ~

■

You cannot change your future,
but you can change your habits, your belief system.
And sure they will change your future
~ Benjamin Franklin ~

■

The only thing that stands between a man and
what he wants from life is often merely the will
to try it and the faith to believe that it is possible
~ Richard Devos ~

Move out of your comfort zone.
You can only grow if you are willing to feel awkward and uncomfortable when you try something new
~ **Brian Tracy** ~

The only devils in the world are
those planted in our hearts & mind.
That's where the battle should be fought
~ Mahatma Gandhi ~

■

Difficulties in your life do not come to destroy you
but to help you realize your hidden potential...
let difficulties know that you are difficult!

■

Many will tell you,
'Quit now, you'll never make it.'
If you disregard that advice, you'll be mostly there
~ David Zucker ~

■

If you desire to blossom like a rose in the garden,
you have to learn the art of adjusting with the thorns

■

Difficult things take a long time;
the impossible takes a little longer

■

If we resist change, we fail.
If we accept change, we survive.
If we create change; we succeed

When I do good, I feel good,
when I do bad, I feel bad. That's my religion
~ Abraham Lincoln ~

You must be the change you wish to see in the world
~ Mahatma Gandhi ~

■

Every achiever that I have heard,
said one thing in common that,
'My life turned around when I began to believe in me'
~ Robert Schuller ~

■

Your chances of success in any
undertaking can always be measured
by your belief in yourself
~ Robert Collier ~

■

I will come again & conquer you,
because as a mountain you can't grow but as a human,
I can
~ Edmund Hillary ~
(after unsuccessful attempts on Everest)

■

There are two primary choices in life:
to accept conditions as they exist,
or accept the responsibility for changing them
~ Denis Waitley ~

Handling Adversity

My experience tells me that when we are in tough times, we learn a lot. Tough times make us think differently and innovate. Success is the result of many failures. In fact, real business building happens in tough times. Many of our own initiatives taken in tough times are highly successful. That's why I once titled my internal communication 'Good times make us strong, bad times make us stronger.' My favourite quote is 'Tough times never last, but tough people do.'

During tough times, the competition is affected by the slowdown and quick decisive action can convert adversity into success. Many initiatives taken during tough times are highly successful. For example, while the competition is into downsizing mode, you can really get good talent.

I feel that without challenges, life becomes very boring. I have seen many firms which were not able to survive adversity and are now history. If we look at the history of successful people, be it Gandhi or Mandela, all have gone through tough challenges.

Success and adversity are two sides of the coin. One cannot exist without the other. Continuous success breeds complacency whereas the occasional failure invites us to spot the opportunity within the adversity that we face.

We must never run away from adversity. We must ask – What is in it for me?

And get something out of it!

Life is a cardiogram. It always
has an up and down graph.
If it is steady it dies

In a day, when you don't come across any problems – you can be sure that you are travelling on the wrong path

~ Swami Vivekananda ~

■

Never confuse a single defeat with a final defeat

~ F. Scott Fitzgerald ~

■

The ultimate measure of a man is not where he stands in moments of comfort and convenience, but where he stands at times of challenge and controversy

~ Martin Luther King ~

■

Smooth seas do not make skillful sailors

~ African proverb ~

■

One's best success comes after one's greatest disappointments

~ Henry Ward Beecher ~

■

Running away from your problems only increases the distance to the solution

The only people with no problems
are dead

Good times make us strong
bad times, stronger

■

You don't become enormously successful
without encountering and overcoming
a number of extremely challenging problems
~ Mark Victor Hansen ~

■

In times of difficulty, some people break down,
while some break records

■

A closed door isn't always locked

■

Without crossing the worst situations...
no one can touch the best corners of life

■

Difficulties strengthen the mind,
as labor does the body
~ Seneca ~

Handling Adversity

Don't be afraid of difficulties.
Greet them, meet them
and beat them!

You must not fight too often with your
enemy or else you will teach him all your tricks of war
~ Napoleon ~

■

Real difficulties can be overcome;
it is only the imaginary ones that are unconquerable
~ Theodore N. Vail ~

■

Our greatest battles are that with our own minds
~ Jameson Frank ~

■

Worry is interest paid on trouble before it is due
~ William R. Inge ~

■

Patience and perseverance have a
magical effect before which
difficulties disappear and obstacles vanish
~ Napoleon Hill ~

Success

Success is the final outcome of our best efforts. I always believe that if I put in my best efforts, I will succeed most of the time.

We can control our efforts, not the outcome. So, success to me is 'best efforts'.

There are no shortcuts to success. Success requires a huge amount of patience, control of our ego and a positive approach. One must be prepared to work hard, and follow our value system.

Some of the things which have worked for me are hard work, sticking to core values, a hunger for knowledge, thinking 'big', taking risks and aligning with like-minded people. Along the way, I grew in self-confidence as I focused on key priorities, became action-oriented, kept on persevering, stayed humble and always listened!

I always feel that a balanced approach works best for sustained success. This approach gives importance to all aspects—health, relationships, career, and knowledge. And to me, success is true success only if it brings happiness.

I think most people have huge untapped potential. Many are not able to tap that potential and turn it into reality. Self-confidence is not only the fuel that makes the fire of potential burn ever so brightly; it is also the spark that ignites the fire in the first place!

Somehow people keep on doubting their capabilities for many reasons. Maybe, they do not have conviction in their ideas. Perhaps, they are not willing to learn. Or they do not want to listen to a lot of negative comments from other people, and hence lose conviction in their own thoughts, ideas or actions.

When I interact with people, I encourage them to understand their own strengths. I motivate them to move on to higher responsibilities; even when they think they are not ready for it. These people do very well. All that I do is to show them the mirror, challenge them to aspire higher in life, and reinforce their strengths and show faith.

The more you push yourself to succeed; the more you do.

A successful man is one who can lay a
firm foundation with the bricks
that others throw at him
~ D. Brinkley ~

We cannot discover new oceans until
we have the courage to lose sight of the shore
~ Muriel Chen ~

■

Success does not depend on making
important decisions quick,
it depends on our quick action on important decisions

■

When you can think of yesterday without regret
& tomorrow without fear, you are
on the road to success
~ Swami Vivekananda ~

■

Fortune favors the brave
~ Publius Terence ~

■

In the confrontation between the stream and the rock,
the stream always wins—
not through strength,
but through persistence
~ Buddha ~

■

The difference between a successful person and
others is not a lack of strength, not a lack of knowledge,
but rather a lack of will
~ Vince Lombardi ~

Success lies not in the result,
but in the effort.
Being the best is not so important,
doing the best is all that matters

Success is ten percent inspiration
and ninety percent perspiration
~ Thomas Edison ~

■

The fact is that successful people
fail far more often than unsuccessful people

■

Successful people think about solutions most of the time.
Unsuccessful people think about problems and
difficulties most of the time

■

You've got to ask. Asking is, in my opinion,
the world's most powerful and
neglected secret to success and happiness
~ Percy Ross ~

■

I cannot give you the formula for success,
but I can give you the formula for failure:
'Try to please everybody'

■

Commit to taking total responsibility for
everything that happens to you.
This one change in thinking has the power
to launch you to the world-class level faster
than any other single idea
~ Steve Siebold ~

I've failed over and over and over
again in my life and that is why
I succeed
~ Michael Jordan ~

People become really quite remarkable
when they start thinking that they can do things.
When they believe in themselves,
they have the first secret of success
~ Norman Vincent Peale ~

■

Talent wins games but teamwork and
intelligence win championships
~ Michael Jordan ~

■

Success is the ability to go from one
failure to another with no loss
of enthusiasm
~ Winston Churchill ~

■

Success in life depends upon two important things:
Vision: Seeing the Invisible &
Mission: Doing the Impossible

■

Life never grows great until it is focused,
dedicated and disciplined

■

Confidence is as vital to success
as oxygen is to the body

Success and excuses do not walk together. If you want to give an excuse forget about success, and if you want success do not give an excuse

Success is nothing more than
a few simple disciplines practiced daily
and failure is nothing more than
a few small errors repeated daily

~ Jim Rohn ~

■

Life takes "passion, determination and skill".
You can't skip any of these three and expect to enjoy
success built to last

~ Condoleezza Rice ~

■

Life is like a play, it is not the length but
the excellence of the acting that matters

~ Seneca ~

■

The greatest waste in the world is the difference between
what we are and what we could become

~ Ben Herbste ~

■

I don't believe in taking right decisions.
I take decisions & then make them right

~ Alexander ~

■

Sooner or later, those who win are those who
think they can

~ Richard Bach ~

Hard Work

I do not believe in luck.

I work very hard. Whether it's my education—becoming a chartered accountant—my health, business, or relationships; I have put in my best efforts in all. That gives me self-satisfaction.

In this complex and competitive world, hardworking people get recognition. They are given their due. However, to work hard does not mean the sheer number of hours. But it means to work on the right activities.

As you go higher the definition of hard work changes. At higher levels, it becomes more of working of the mind—intellect, analytical rigor; rather than physical action. Many people argue for smart work as opposed to hard work. In my opinion, it is a combination of both.

When I start my yoga session, it is hard. It's tough to begin, but when I finish, I feel very different and charged up. Hard work causes pain at the start, but it gives disproportionate gains in the long term.

Concentrate all your thoughts upon the
work at hand.
The sun's rays do not burn until
brought to a focus
~ Alexander Graham Bell ~

I 'm a great believer in luck, and I find the
harder I work the more I have of it
~ Thomas Jefferson ~

■

It's true that every effort is not converted into success,
but it's equally true that success
does not come without effort

■

Hard work is like a staircase and luck is like a lift.
The lift may fail but, the staircase is sure
to take you to the top

■

Do the hard jobs first. The easy jobs will
take care of themselves
~ Dale Carnegie ~

■

You can't get disproportionate gains without
disproportionate pain

■

I am not afraid of a fighter who knows
a thousand kicks, but I am
afraid of the one who has practiced
one kick a thousand times
~ Bruce Lee ~

Hard Work

Hard work pays off in the future, laziness gives instant benefits

Victory is always at our feet; but the problem
is we are too lazy to bend

■

You cannot harvest what you did not sow

■

Persistence: The arrow that hits the bull's
eye is the result of one
hundred misses
~ A Buddhist proverb ~

■

Efforts may fail. But don't fail to
make efforts

■

Nothing can take the place of persistence.
Talent will not; nothing is more common
than unsuccessful men with talent.
Genius will not; unrewarded genius is almost a proverb.
Education will not; the world is full of educated derelicts.
Persistence and determination alone are omnipotent
~ Calvin Coolidge ~

Values

In my opinion, values are lived rather than talked about. You either live up to them or you don't. There is no in-between. In fact, many times, living up to values can make us face temporary setbacks and test our nerves; but it always gives us a good night's sleep.

Values earn trust and respect. And living up to them skyrockets our self-esteem.

There are no shortcuts to success in life. In this 'success-at-all-costs' world, many people compromise on their values; but they do not go far. Whether it is paying taxes or being transparent with customers, associates or family members, values will make us trustworthy. It is my strong conviction that following the right value system gives you tremendous competitive advantage at the individual and organizational level.

I have seen that people who compromise on their values get short-term benefits, but in the long run, they are the biggest losers. Their greed doesn't take them far.

If you live your values you will live a highly satisfying life.

In stock markets there is huge price premium on the companies who abide by values. The Tata Group, Infosys, Wipro and many other groups are known for their values. There are many other companies/ groups whom markets don't respect because of their values.

Take charge of your life, otherwise somebody else will

The difference between ability & character-ability will get us to the top, character will keep us there

■

Courage is the mastery of fear, not the absence of fear

~ Mark Twain ~

■

You must not lose faith in humanity.
Humanity is an ocean;
if a few drops of the ocean are dirty,
the ocean does not become dirty

~ Mahatma Gandhi ~

■

Everyone knows how to count,
but very few know what counts!

■

If we have integrity, nothing else matters.
if we don't have integrity, anything else matters

~ Alan Simpson ~

■

If you do not have courage, you may not have an opportunity to use any of your other virtues

~ Samuel Johnson ~

■

Honesty is the cornerstone of all success, without which confidence and ability to perform shall cease to exist

Forgiveness is an act of love and kindness, not of justice

Goodness is the only investment that never
fails to return a dividend

■

Motivation gets you started. Habits keep you running.
Attitude decides your pace and
values decide your destination

■

There is sufficiency in the world for man's needs
but not for man's greed
~ Mahatma Gandhi ~

■

The regrets we should have is not for the
wrong things we did; but for the right things
we could have done but never did

■

Hurt me with the truth but never comfort me with a lie
~ Swami Vivekananda ~

■

When you settle for mediocrity in the small things,
you will also begin to settle for mediocrity in the big things

■

If you like me, raise your hands.
If not, then raise your standards
~ Warren Buffet ~

Knowledge

For the last 15-17 years my favorite reading time has been between 5-6 am everyday and lots of time over the weekends. In fact, my wife often inquires whether books are my first wife or the second! That one hour out of twenty four hours is the most productive and fulfilling for me. I have read hundreds of books and articles this way.

And the book I am sharing with you is the result of my reading. One has many things to read; but should select what to read based on their own passion, liking and areas of interest.

Though I am in the stock-market, I don't read books on markets and investing. I read on leadership, management, and self-motivation. I love to read about great lives—their biographies are very inspiring and insightful.

I think this hunger for knowledge is the biggest differentiating factor in today's cut-throat competitive world. Even after reading so many books, I feel there is a long way to go. I also learn a lot on the job by interacting with people at all levels, including customers; and asking the right questions. I learn in seminars and training workshops.

Knowledge is the one thing that grows when you share it. So I make it a point to share many books, extracts and articles with my team, friends, family and peers.

Unless updated or shared, knowledge becomes obsolete. It has to keep pace with changing times. The past few centuries have been of Goddess Lakshmi (wealth). The coming centuries will belong to Goddess Saraswati (knowledge).

The road to Goddess Lakshmi passes through the gates of Goddess Saraswati.

You have to learn lessons from other's mistakes, because you may not get the time to commit all the mistakes yourself

If I had nine hours to chop down a tree,
I'd spend the first six sharpening my axe
~ Abraham Lincoln ~

■

The man who does not read good books
has no advantage over the man
who can't read them
~ Mark Twain ~

■

Nine-tenths of wisdom is being
wise in time
~ Theodore Roosevelt ~

■

When you give excellent
education to your children,
wonders happen!

■

Readers are leaders and
leaders are readers

■

Reading is to the mind
what exercise is to the body

An investment in knowledge
always pays the best interest
~ Benjamin Franklin ~

The more we study, the more
we discover our ignorance
~ Percy Bysshe Shelley ~

■

It is a thousand times better to have
common sense without an education
than to have an education without common sense
~ Robert Green Ingersoll ~

■

I believe people should study a little
bit every day. It should become
habitual, like brushing your teeth,
combing your hair, having
a shower or getting dressed
~ Bob Proctor ~

■

The school is not the end but only
the beginning of an education
~ Calvin Coolidge ~

■

The man who learns nothing
from the past will be punished by the future

The difference between intelligence and stupidity is that intelligence has a limit

The illiterate of the 21st century will
not be those who cannot read and write,
but those who cannot learn, unlearn, and relearn
~ Alvin Toffler ~

■

A man of wealth has many enemies,
while a man of knowledge has many friends

■

Knowledge becomes obsolete every few years.
If you don't renew your knowledge
often and thoroughly,
you become obsolete and fall behind
~ Peter Drucker ~

■

People respect you not for the knowledge you have,
but the way you utilize it
~ Albert Einstein ~

■

The ability to convert ideas to things
is the secret to outward success
~ Henry Ward Beecher ~

■

People don't resist change.
They resist being changed
~ Peter Senge ~

Life's tragedy is that we get old too soon and wise too late

~ Benjamin Franklin ~

In reading the lives of great men, I found
that the first victory they won was over themselves.
Self-discipline with all of them came first
~ Harry Truman ~

■

There are essentially two things that will
make us wiser: the books we read and
the people we meet
~ Charles Jones ~

■

One of the paradoxes of the world is that stupid ones
are damn sure about
everything, and intelligent ones are full of
doubts about anything!
~ Bertrand Russell ~

■

Surround yourself with successful people.
You are the average of the five people
you spend the most time with
~ Jim Rohn ~

■

We should be greedy about knowledge

■

The trouble with most people is that they think
with their hopes and fears rather than their minds

Action

Let me share an anecdote. Three frogs are sitting on a large rock. Two decide to jump. So, how many frogs are left on the rock? One, right? Wrong! Just because two frogs decide does not mean they do! There is a gap between decision and action. Knowing and doing are different things. Successful, high-energy people are good at both. They have a strong bias for action.

In interviews, I ask, 'Are you good in strategy or execution?' Most smart guys say, they are good in both! Then I ask where you are better at? This, they find difficult to answer.

One of the best books I have read about execution is by Ram Charan and it is called 'Execution'.

Execution differentiates successful and failing organizations. At the end of the day, it is the right actions which lead to results. An average strategy excellently executed is a far better option than an excellent strategy with average execution. Once you are in action mode, there will be many challenges. But till date no other route to success has been found. Action is the only way!

In my company we put a huge premium on people who are action-oriented.

When there is a mountain to climb, waiting and watching will not make it small

Well done is better than well said
~ Benjamin Franklin ~

■

The best time to plant a tree was 20 years back;
the second best time is today

■

An average plan vigorously executed is far better than
a brilliant plan on which nothing is done
~ Brian Tracy ~

■

Knowing is not enough; we must apply.
Willing is not enough; we must do
~ Johann Wolfgang von Goethe ~

■

Action is the foundational key to
all success
~ Anthony Robbins ~

■

Life is like riding a bicycle. You don't fall off
unless you stop pedaling

There are two kinds of people –
those of words and those of deeds

If you stop every time a dog barks,
your road will never end
~ Arabian proverb ~

■

The world is not a parking lot,
it's a racing track.
Keep on moving

■

If everything's under control, you're going too slow
~ Mario Andretti ~

■

Take the first step in faith.
You don't have to see the whole staircase.
Just take the first step
~ Martin Luther King Jr. ~

■

Losers let it happen.
Winners make it happen
~ Denis Waitley ~

■

An idea that is developed and
put into action is more important
than an idea that exists only as an idea
~ Buddha ~

There are two times in a man's life when he should not speculate: when he cannot afford it and when he can

~ Mark Twain ~

Nothing would be done at all if one waited until
one could do it so well that no
one could find fault with it
~ John Henry Newman ~

■

It is not the 'deficiency of knowledge',
but 'the efficiency of execution'
that separates achievers from the rest!

■

Ships are safest in the harbor but they are not meant to be there. They have to sail long, hard and face stormy seas to reach the comfort of a desirable destination

■

Words are mere bubbles of water, but deeds
are drops of gold
~ Chinese proverb ~

■

You will learn more about a road by travelling it,
rather than consulting all the maps in the world

■

Direction is more important than speed.
We are so busy looking at our speedometers,
that we often miss milestones on the way

If you really want to do something,
you'll find a way.
If you don't,
you'll find an excuse

We must think big and act bigger

■

The people who get on this world are the people who get up and look for the circumstances they want and if they can't find them, make them

~ George Bernard Shaw ~

■

People may doubt what you say,
but they will always believe
what you do

■

If your actions inspire others
to dream more, learn more,
do more and become more, you are a leader!

~ John Quincy ~

■

I hear and I forget.
I see and I remember.
I do and I understand

~ Chinese proverb ~

Only while sleeping one makes
no mistakes
~ Ingvar Kamprad ~

You miss one hundred percent of the shots
you don't take
~ Wayne Gretsky ~

■

If the first button of a shirt is wrongly put,
all the rest are surely crooked.
So always be careful on your first step

■

The journey of a thousand miles begins
with a single step
~ Lao Tzu ~

■

The time is always right to do what is right
~ Martin Luther King, Jr. ~

■

If you know you are doing the right things,
just relax and perform.
Forget about the outcome.
You can't control anything anyway
~ Michael Jordan ~

■

Patience in planning and impatience in
execution always creates miracles

I prefer attitude over skills as attitude cannot be learnt; but skills can be. I always use attitude as a gate-keeping measure when I recruit persons or when I give higher responsibilities. People of average or even below average potential but with a great attitude can work magic with their sheer attitude! A super talent with a poor attitude sinks to the abyss, taking others along with him.

People with the right and positive attitude always rise higher in life. They assume full responsibility for their actions and consequences. They focus on solutions, and not problems.

I have seen families' break-up, friends being parted, organizations fall apart because of a problem with attitude. Ego comes in between.

The average player with the right attitude will always win over the talented player with attitude problems; who operates in a silo.

Indeed, I have found people going places with the right attitude. Positive attitude is like a magnet drawing like-minded people, creating bonds, forming strong win-win relationships.

Only passion, great passion,
can elevate the soul to great things
~ Denis Diderot ~

I never did a day's work in my life. It was all fun

~ Thomas Edison ~

■

The quality of a person's life is in direct proportion to their commitment to excellence, regardless of their chosen field of endeavor

~ Vince Lombardi ~

■

You will see it when you believe it

~ Wayne Dyer ~

■

The height of your accomplishments will equal the depth of your convictions

~ William F Scholavion ~

■

The future belongs to those who believe in the beauty of their dreams

~ Eleanor Roosevelt ~

■

The only disability in life is a bad attitude

~ Scott Hamilton ~

Effort only fully releases its reward
after a person refuses to quit
~ Napoleon Hill ~

It's a funny thing about life; if you refuse
to accept anything but the best,
you very often get it
~ W. Somerset Maugham ~

■

When you think positive,
it happens! when you think negative, it happens too!

■

Ego is a double-edged sword
which cuts popularity, in the outer world and
purity in the inner world

■

If you worry about a trouble
it becomes double. But when you smile at it,
it disappears like a bubble

■

One thing I like about stones that
come in my way is, once I pass across them,
they automatically become my milestones
~ Swami Vivekananda ~

With a bad attitude you can never have a positive day and with a positive attitude you can never have a bad day

A quitter never wins and a winner never quits
~ Napolean Hill ~

■

Everyone thinks of changing the world,
but no one thinks of changing himself
~ Leo Tolstoy ~

■

Mediocre people first see and then believe;
wise people first believe and then see

■

A strong and positive attitude creates more miracles
than any other thing because...
life is 10% how you make it and 90% how you take it

■

Of all the "attitudes" we can acquire,
surely the attitude of gratitude is the most important
and by far the most life-changing

■

We can't have all that we desire,
but we will get all that we deserve

Ninety percent of all failures
come from people who have a habit of
making excuses
~ George Washington Carver ~

The people who accept criticism
are the people who are genuinely interested
in self-improvement

■

The pessimist sees difficulty in every opportunity.
The optimist sees opportunity in every difficulty
~ Winston Churchill ~

■

The business race will be won not by those
who run the fastest, but by those who last the longest

■

One machine can do the work of fifty ordinary men.
No machine can do the work of one extraordinary man
~ Elbert Hubbard ~

■

Those who take more chances and dare to do
more than others, will naturally
experience more failures

■

If someone feels that they had never made a mistake
in their life, then it means they had never tried
a new thing in their life
~ Albert Einstein ~

We will either find a way or make one
~ Hannibal ~

Life doesn't provide warranties and guarantees.
It only provides possibilities and opportunities!

■

It is better to light a candle than to curse the darkness
~ Eleanor Roosevelt ~

■

I had the blues because I had no shoes,
until upon the street;
I met a man who had no feet
~ Denis Waitley ~

■

Expect the best, plan for the worst
and prepare to be surprised
~ Dennis Waitley ~

■

The price of discipline is always
less than the pain of regret
~ Swami Vivekananda ~

Impossible is not a fact...
It's an opinion

There are no mistakes, only experiences.
There are no problems, only challenges

■

Life is an echo, it all comes back.
The good, the bad, the false, the true.
So give the world the best you have and the best will come back to you

■

Man wishes to fly like a bird,
sing like a cuckoo, dance like a peacock,
swim like a fish,
but man does not wish to live like a man
~ Swami Vivekanada ~

■

Feeling sorry for yourself,
and your present condition,
is not only a waste of energy but
the worst habit you could possibly have
~ Dale Carnegie ~

■

A fool becomes intelligent!
when he understands that he's a fool!
A genius becomes a fool when he believes that he's a genius

The size of man can be measured
by the size of the thing that
makes him angry
~ Rabindranath Tagore ~

Whether you think you can or whether
you think you can't, you're right
~ Henry Ford ~

■

To be yourself in a world that is constantly
trying to make you something else is the greatest
accomplishment
~ Ralph Waldo Emerson ~

■

Yesterday I was clever so I wanted to change the world.
Today I am wise so I am changing myself

■

Holding on to anger is like keeping
a burning piece of coal in your hands
to throw at your enemy, but it burns you first
~ Buddha ~

■

No one can make you feel inferior without your consent
~ Eleanor Roosevelt ~

■

For every minute you are angry with someone,
you lose 60 seconds of happiness
that you can never get back

Time Management

God is very fair and democratic. He has given 24 hours to every human being. But some people break records, and some people break themselves and cause self-destruct.

One tool which I have found to be very important is Pareto's law, that is prioritizing your activities and investing maximum time on high-impact activities. Stephen Covey in his book, Seven Habits of Highly Effective People has talked about the 'urgent' v/s the 'important'.

I try to spend 5-10 minutes everyday to plan for the next day, and also take out time to plan the entire week at a stretch. This is the most productive action for me.

You must plan your time in such a way that you set aside time for your own health and family. In fact, if I were to have just one training program for everyone on my team, it will be on time management. That's how critical it is. I have seen that small, trivial activities eat away time of most people and hold them back from tackling higher priorities. Telephone calls, emails, social networking sites, meetings – all turn out to be timewasters if we do not put them under the microscope.

This is where leaders are differentiated from others. They are productive and wisely utilize their time. This vital trait alone separates the men from the boys. Think of any successful person and you will find out that he or she is extremely good at time management. The unsuccessful ones will always cite lack of time as a cover up.

I plan my daily schedule such that the most important assignments and meetings are in most productive first half of the day, while regular items are scheduled in the second half. I maintain a list of pending action-points with priority assigned to each.

My most 'looked forward to' time is between 5 and 6 am, when I read followed by exercise time from 6 to 7 am. This routine which I have followed for the last 15-17 years is the best start to the day for me.

Time Management

The quickest way to do so many things is
to do only one thing at
a time
~ Chanakya ~

"The time to repair the roof is when
the sun is shining

~ John F. Kennedy ~

■

We are focused so much on
today's problems that we put off
planning for tomorrow's opportunities

■

The bad news is time flies. The good news is
you are the pilot

~ Michael Alshuler ~

■

Your time is limited, so don't waste it
living someone else's life

~ Steve Jobs ~

■

The person who tries to do everything,
accomplishes nothing

■

Our success will be largely determined by our ability
to concentrate single-mindedly on one thing at a time

~ Brian Tracy ~

Early to bed and early to rise
makes a person
healthy, wealthy and wise

Take an interest in the future –
that's where you are going to spend
the rest of your life
~ Mark Twain ~

■

The telephone is one of the most effective time savers
and also one of the biggest time wasters

■

When you're really busy, you don't have much energy
to think of other things even
if they're the things that matter most

■

If your priorities don't get put into your planner,
other peoples' priorities will get put into your planner

■

Many people are so busy driving that
they don't have time to stop for gas

■

You control your life by controlling your time
~ Hyrum W. Smith ~

Until we can manage time, we can manage nothing else

- Peter F. Drucker

Don't say you don't have enough time.
You have exactly the same number of hours per day
that were given to
Helen Keller, Pasteur, Michelangelo, Mother Teresa,
Leonardo da Vinci, Thomas Jefferson and Albert Einstein
~ H. Jackson Brown ~

■

We can't have a better tomorrow
if we are thinking about yesterday all the time

■

Much of the stress that people feel
doesn't come from having too much to do.
It comes from not finishing what they started
~ David Allen ~

■

When I am anxious it is because I am living in the future.
When I am depressed it is because I am living in the past.

■

When time never stops for us,
then why do we always wait for time.
No time is wrong to do the right things

One of the greatest enemies that we can ever face in life is, the illusion that there will be more time tomorrow than today

We always overestimate what we can do in one year
but underestimate what we can do in 5 years
~ Peter Drucker ~

■

A good plan of today is better
than a great plan of tomorrow

■

Everything is easy when you are busy,
but nothing is easy when you are lazy
~ Swami Vivekananda ~

■

All work and no rest takes the spring and
bound out of the most vigorous life.
Time spent in judicious resting
is not time wasted, but time gained
~ M. B. Grier ~

■

Those who make the worst use of their time are the
first to complain of its shortness
~ Jean de la Bruyere ~

■

We all find time to do what we really want to do
~ William Feather ~

Appreciation

8+4=12

5+9=14

2+14=16

5+7=13

(Read the four sums above and comment)

99% people will conclude that the last one is the wrong statistic. We are always in fault-finding mode.

Three sums are right. One is wrong. But most people will mention only the wrong.

There is a huge need for appreciation in our highly stressed world. Appreciation is such a powerful tool for relationships! Human beings love being complimented, appreciated, and their strengths being pointed out. They love simple words of appreciation like 'Thank you', 'Keep it up'. They become motivated and charged to do better. We ought to overcome the mind set of a fault-finding person. We must catch people 'doing the right things' rather than just 'doing things right' and applaud them!

But somewhere we are stingy, about using appreciative words. As Mother Teresa said, "There is more hunger in the world for love and appreciation; than for bread." Our world is witness to so many conflicts and fights. There is lack of trust because people are always in the fault-finding mode, on ego trips and in the battle to prove that they are right.

Children also require words of encouragement and appreciation to bring out their potential. I have seen many times that parents focus too much on the perceived weaknesses and deficiencies. This dents the child's confidence and stunts the child's growth. So many talents have been lost in this world due to this self-defeating mindset.

A word of appreciation is like a magic elixir for improving performance.

Appreciation

There are two things to aim for in life;
first to get what you want,
and after that to enjoy it. Only the wisest of
mankind achieve the second
~ Logan Pearsall Smith ~

Everyone has an invisible sign hanging from their neck
saying, 'Make me feel important'
~ Mary Kay Ash ~

■

There is more hunger in this world
for love and appreciation than for bread
~ Mother Teresa ~

■

Don't compare yourself with anyone in this world.
If you do so, you are insulting yourself
~ Alen Strike ~

■

Look for the good in every person and every situation.
You'll almost always find it
~ Brian Tracy ~

■

Take your work seriously, but never yourself
~ Margot Fonteyn ~

A day without laughter
is a day wasted
~ Charlie Chaplin ~

Humor is by far the most significant activity
of the human brain
~ Edward De Bono ~

■

We must accept finite disappointment,
but must never lose infinite hope
~ Martin Luther King ~

■

Most people overestimate their problems
and underestimate their potential

■

Competitors and critics are our partners for our
improvement and growth. Always thank and bless them

■

It takes a strong person to say sorry,
and an even stronger person to forgive

■

I can go on for two months on one compliment
~ Mark Twain ~

Appreciation

If we did all the things we are capable of,
we would literally astound ourselves
~ Thomas Edison~

A word of encouragement during failure,
is worth more than an hour of praise when you succeed

■

Praise loudly
blame softly

■

Giving criticism requires compassion,
insight and tact
~ Patti Hathaway ~

■

Many receive advice, only the wise profit by it
~ Publilius Syrus ~

■

Patience and politeness is not a person's weakness,
it is a reflection of a person's inner strength

■

My whole effort here is to pull my people
away from the past and the future
and just make them available to the
intense beauty of the present
~ Osho ~

Communication

We live in an over-communicated society—television channels with all their content, advertising, mobile calls and messages, emails, social networking sites, etc.

The more the mechanisms, the less we understand that right communication might mean less, but focused communication.

But here we are. We want to talk more and listen less. We want to read more but understand less. We want to question more and answer less. We want to use powerful strong language, but less sweet words.

We have lots of time to be on the phone but we don't have time to be with our spouse or children in person. We have time for our happy customers, but no time to spare for the unhappy ones. We are ever-ready to offer advice to a lot of associates, but no time to listen to their feedback.

But there are people who know how to use communication skills to their advantage. Public speaking is a critical skill to master for any budding leader. Being excellent in oral and written communication is a precondition for success. Another important skill is to have a style of communication that has humor. Words spoken with a smile will always bring better results.

In my experience, face-to-face communication is more important than any other communication. This is because the tone, the body language, the words—all can be perceived directly in face-to-face communication.

We also need to be aware of the biases that creep in to our communication. Such bias distorts our communication and leads to gaps in understanding.

Communication is the bridge that helps build relationships.

Courtesy costs nothing
but pays well

Two things indicate our weakness:
To be silent when it is proper to speak!
And to speak when it is proper to be silent!

■

When someone criticizes us,
it's time to evaluate ourselves.
When someone praises us,
its time to evaluate them!

■

Be careful in your thoughts when you are alone and be careful in your words when you are in a crowd

■

The most important thing in communication is to hear what isn't being said
~ Peter Drucker ~

■

It takes three years to learn how to use the tongue, but a lifetime to learn where and when to use it appropriately

■

You can tell whether a man is clever by his answers.
You can tell whether a man is wise by his questions
~ Naquib Mahfouz ~

The real art of conversation is not only to say
the right thing in the right place,
but also to leave unsaid the wrong thing at the
tempting moment
~ Dorothy Nevill ~

Never underestimate the power of your tongue.
If not held tight and managed properly,
this softest organ of your body could be
responsible for the hardest phase of your life

■

One constructive suggestion is worth a
hundred complaints

■

Your success over a lifetime will be more
directly linked to your writing and speaking skills
~ Peter Drucker ~

■

Most of us would rather be ruined by praise
than saved by criticism
~ Norman Vincent Peale ~

■

When the eyes say one thing and the tongue another,
a practical man relies on the language of the first
~ Ralph Waldo Emerson ~

In true dialogue, both sides are willing to change

Good presentations have a persuasive opening and killer closing. In the middle, you find a body supported by powerful stories, facts, exercises and quotes
~ Lorri Vaughter Allen ~

■

Silence and smiles are two powerful tools.
A smile is the way to solve many problems
and silence is the way to avoid many problems

■

If your eyes are sweet you will like all
people of the world, but if your tongue is sweet,
all the people of the world will like you

■

Argument is bad.
But discussion is good.
Arguments find out 'who' is right.
Discussions find out 'what' is right

■

When we have the ability to listen to
almost anything without losing our
temper or confidence, we are truly educated

Conversation is an exercise
of the brain. Gossip is a brainless exercise
of the tongue

~ Chanakya ~

Politeness costs nothing and buys everything
~ Mary Worthy Montagu ~

■

A smile is the lighting system of face,
cooling system of heart,
sparkling system of eyes,
and relaxing system of mind!

■

Always try to prove that you are right.
But never attempt to prove that others are wrong

■

To be kind is more important than to be right;
often people need a patient heart that listens,
not a brilliant mind that speaks

■

When we argue unnecessarily,
we lose our power of judgement

■

The funny part of communication:
We listen half, understand quarter and speak double!!

Make sure you have finished speaking
before the audience has finished listening
~ Dorothy Sarnoff ~

90% of life's problems are due to the
tone of voice. It is not what we say,
it is how we say it that creates problems

■

Kind words can be short and easy to speak,
but their echoes are truly endless
~ Mother Teresa ~

■

Speeches are like babies –
easy to conceive but hard to deliver

■

Blunt people make the most
pointed remarks

■

Wise men talk because they have something to say;
fools because they have to say something
~ Plato ~

■

A slip of the foot you may soon recover,
but a slip of the tongue you may never get over
~ Benjamin Franklin ~

Communication

Think before you speak...
but never speak
all you think

The right word spoken at the right time
sometimes achieves miracles
~ Josef Goebbels ~

■

A speech without a specific purpose is like a journey
without a destination
~ Ralph C Smedley ~

■

The most valuable of all talents is that of never using
two words when one will do
~ Thomas Jefferson ~

■

Hard words can't touch any soft heart,
but soft words can touch any hard heart

■

Don't raise your voice.
Improve the quality of your arguments

■

Our speaking is well shaped and sharpened
by our reading as well as our listening

Most people see what they want to see and they hear what they want to hear

Speak when you are angry and you will
make the best speech you will ever regret
~ Ambrose Bierce ~

■

Silent lips may avoid many problems.
But smiling lips will solve most problems

■

Knowledge speaks, but wisdom listens
~ Jimi Hendrix ~

■

God has given us two ears and
one mouth for a reason –
to listen twice and then to speak

■

Mere silence is not wisdom.
For wisdom consists in knowing when and
how to speak and when to keep silent
~ J P Camus ~

■

Speak sweetly, if you need to eat your
words, they don't taste bad.
~ Chanakya ~

You're not fully dressed until you wear a smile

If one can listen to others without likes,
dislikes, anger, greed or prejudice,
wordless wisdom starts flowing into our lives

■

When you talk, you are only repeating
what you already know. But if you listen,
you may learn something new

■

Always speak tasty words in your life
as you never know when you will have to eat them

■

Look out for the tongue; it's in a wet place and might slip

■

During arguments, intelligent people use
silence and stupid people use their tongue.
During discussions, intelligent people use their tongue
and stupid people use silence

■

Never argue with idiots.
Because first they bring you to their level
and then they beat you with their experience

Social Responsibility

We should be grateful to our elders and the society for the invaluable legacy of knowledge, culture and heritage. This legacy has continually revitalized our civilization through the ages.

If society has given you everything that you desired; shouldn't you ask the question, "What can I give back?"

I feel it is my duty to give something back to society without expectation of any return.

I have seen lots of people donate money, but they ask for something in return. That is business, not charity.

There are many present-day challenges–poverty, education, health, etc.

I believe that instead of temples, the world would be a better place if we do everything possible to satisfy and fulfill basic human needs.

There are so many institutions; NGOs, civil-society groups, dedicated social activists, who are rendering invaluable service to the entire world. Enlightened corporate groups like the Tatas, Birlas, and Wipro are beacons of corporate social responsibility. They work for the greater common good knowing that a sustainable world where basic human needs are fulfilled is the only way to ensure global peace, wellbeing and prosperity.

There is nothing as satisfying as giving back.

Give more and you'll have more
~ Hyrum W. Smith ~

A candle loses nothing of its light
by lighting another candle

■

Do what you can, with what you have,
right where you are
~ Theodore Roosevelt ~

■

There are two kinds of people in the world:
Givers and Takers.
The takers may eat better, but the givers sleep better
~ Mother Teresa ~

■

To give service to a single heart by a single act is better
than a thousand heads bowing in prayer
~ Mahatma Gandhi ~

■

If you cannot be a pencil to write anyone's happiness,
try at least to be a nice rubber to erase everyone's sorrows!

■

Too often we underestimate the power of a touch,
a small word, a listening ear, an honest compliment or
the smallest act of caring—all of which have the potential
to turn a life around.
~ Leo Buscaglia ~

■

Don't judge each day by the harvest you reap but by the
seeds that you plant
~ R L Stevenson ~

You do 100 good things nobody remembers, you do one thing wrong nobody forgets

Dividing an elephant in half does not
produce two small elephants
~ Peter Senge ~

■

To avoid criticism, do nothing, say nothing, be nothing
~ Elbert Hubbard ~

■

People are not useless, they are used less

■

'Truth' is a debit card—pay first and use later
'Lie' is a credit card—use first and pay later

■

What gets measured gets done,
what gets measured and feedbacked gets done well,
what gets rewarded gets repeated
~ John E. Jones ~

■

Motivate those around you and they will eventually live up to the expectations. Put them down and they have no reason to be any better

■

Life is an 'Echo'. What you send out, comes back

■

Tomorrow to me is an unopened gift.
I savour the unpredictability of it all
~ Vivek Oberoi ~

Patience is a bitter plant but it has a sweet fruit

~ German proverb ~

When you are right, there's no need to be angry,
When you are wrong, you have no right to be angry

■

If you are patient in one moment of anger,
you will escape a hundred days of sorrow
~ Chinese proverb ~

■

As long as we don't 'forgive' others,
they occupy 'rent free' space in our mind

■

Great things are not done by impulse,
but by a series of small things brought together
~ Vincent van Gogh ~

■

Some of the biggest problems arise when we begin to believe
that we are perfect or that the world should be perfect
~ Leo Buscaglia ~

■

I have lived a long life and had many troubles,
most of which never happened
~ Mark Twain ~

■

People who value their privileges above their principles
soon lose both

■

Excuses are the easiest things to manufacture,
and the hardest things to sell